Treasury of Secrets

Featuring The Secret Princess, The Tinder Box and Rumpelstiltskin

igloobooks

The Secret Princess

Once upon a time, in a kingdom far, far away, lived a beautiful Princess named Amelia. She was very pretty, with tumbling blonde curls and large brown eyes.

The Queen adored Princess Amelia and showed her daughter how to sing the sweetest songs, how to grow the prettiest flowers and how to cook the tastiest soup. But, one day, there was great sadness in the palace. The Queen had died.

Because the King loved Princess Amelia so much, he wanted only the best for her. He hunted throughout the land to find a new wife. Soon, the King announced he was to be married again.

"Now you've got a new mother," the King said happily to the Princess, after his wedding.

The Princess' new stepmother smiled coldly. As she gazed at her stepdaughter's youth and beauty, her heart burned with jealousy.

Early one morning, the stepmother woke Princess Amelia. She grabbed the Princess roughly by the arm and pulled her out of bed.

"You're coming with me," the stepmother hissed. "You will leave this kingdom and never return."

The Princess was taken to the stepmother's large country house. It was far away from anywhere and the only people living there were servants, who weren't friendly.

The stepmother took the Princess into the kitchens and dragged her up to the cook.

"Amelia, you'll work as a kitchen maid," the Princess' stepmother said. "Cook will tell you what to do." And, with that, she strode out of the kitchen, leaving the Princess behind.

"Make some supper," Cook ordered.

"But I don't know how," the Princess protested. "All I can make is my mother's soup."

"Then make soup," Cook said, sinking down into a comfortable chair in front of the fire. "I've been working my fingers to the bone for years. Now it's your turn."

When the stepmother returned to the kingdom, she took the King aside.

"I'm afraid I have bad news. Your daughter has run away and she's nowhere to be found," she said.

The King was heartbroken. He did not know how he would live without his lovely daughter.

Once again, the palace was filled with sadness.

Many months passed. Princess Amelia's days were always the same. She'd wake early in her small, damp attic room and put on her grey, ragged servant's clothes. Then she would make soup, clean the kitchen and sweep the house from top to bottom. Only after she'd finished all her jobs was she allowed into the garden, where she'd care for the flowers and plants that grew there. Being outside in the garden made the Princess happy and, when she was happy, she sang.

The Princess sang in the spring, as she tended to the bulbs and buds unfurled on the trees. She sang in the summer, as the flowers bloomed and the sun warmed her skin. She sang in the autumn, as the leaves changed their shades and fell to the ground. She even sang in the winter, as she cleared a blanket of snow from the earth.

One day, a Prince was passing on his horse when he heard Princess Amelia's delightful voice singing a haunting melody. It was the sweetest sound he'd ever heard. "The owner of such a voice must be incredibly beautiful," the Prince thought. "I must find out who she is."

The Prince climbed down from his horse and peered through the hedge, trying to see who was singing. But the hedge was very thick and the Prince could not see more than a glimpse of pink rags and a flash of blonde hair.

The Prince rode up to the front of the house and knocked at the door. When Cook saw the Prince, her eyes widened with delight. She'd never met such a handsome man before.

"Good afternoon," the Prince said politely. "I've been traveling for many hours and was wondering if I could trouble you for something to eat?"

"Of course," Cook beamed. "I'll bring you some food immediately."

When Cook returned, she placed a bowl of the Princess' soup in front of the Prince. The servants watched as he ate a spoonful then licked his lips.

"This is the best soup I've ever tasted," the Prince said. When the Prince had finished his meal, he sat back in his chair. "Who is the maiden singing in the garden?" he asked.

The servants all looked at each other. Their mistress had warned them they would be punished if they spoke to anyone about Princess Amelia.

"There's nobody in the garden," Cook lied.

"Yes, there is," the Prince said. "She has the most beautiful voice in the world. Won't you tell me who she is?"

"Sir, you are mistaken," Cook insisted. "There's nobody here but us. It must have been a bird singing."

Disappointed, the Prince left the house and rode away on his horse.

"You're forbidden to go outside anymore," Cook said to Princess Amelia. Instead, after the Princess had finished her chores, she was banished to the attic room.

The Prince returned again and again to the house. Not only did he long for more of the delicious soup, he yearned to discover the identity of the maiden who'd sung so sweetly in the garden. But there was no sign of her and the Prince never heard the song again.

Although Princess Amelia was upset at being kept inside, she refused to feel sad. She was a kind and happy girl who enjoyed helping the other servants with their work. As more time passed, all of the servants, even Cook, grew to like Princess Amelia.

One day, when the familiar knock on the door came, Cook entered the kitchen. "Amelia, the Prince is waiting in the dining room," she said. "Why don't you take him his soup today?"

"Of course, Cook," the Princess said. She spooned the soup carefully into a bowl and sang as she carried it upstairs.

As the Prince heard the singing, his heart leaped. Finally, he would discover who had such a delightful voice. As Princess Amelia walked in, the Prince immediately fell in love. The girl was as lovely as her song.

"Please, won't you join me," the Prince said, as he took his soup.

As the Prince ate, they talked and talked. After the last drop of soup disappeared, the Prince took the Princess' hand in his.

"I wish to marry you," he said. "You are the most wonderful person I've ever met. But it seems fate is against us, for I can only marry the daughter of a King."

"But I am the daughter of a King!" Princess Amelia exclaimed with pleasure. She explained about her past and how she had been banished by her evil stepmother.

The Prince was delighted. "In that case, we shall be married tomorrow," he declared. He took the Princess by the hand and whisked her away to his palace.

The Prince informed Princess Amelia's father, who was joyfully reunited with his beloved daughter on her wedding day.

Soon, Princess Amelia had a large garden of her own to care for and was so happy she sang all day for her husband, the Prince.

The Tinder Box

One day, a young soldier returning from a war met an old woman on a lonely country road.

"Hello, young man," greeted the old woman, cheerily. "I've got a question for you. Tell me," she asked, would you like to take home with you as much money as you could carry?"

"Of course I would. Who wouldn't?" laughed the soldier.

"If you follow my instructions, you will be able to do just that," said the old woman. The soldier was surprised by the woman's words but, having nothing better to do, decided to listen further.

First of all, the old woman took off her apron and gave it to the soldier. Then she told him that if he were to climb down into the hollow of the nearby tree, at the bottom he would find three doors. Behind the first door lay chests that were full of bronze coins, but there was a dog with eyes as big as saucers guarding them.
If he lay the apron on the ground, the dog would sit on it and he could then stuff his pockets with the bronze coins.

Behind the second door was a room full of silver coins. There was also a dog guarding this room, and this dog had eyes as big as mill wheels!
If he lay the apron on the ground again, this dog would also sit on it and he could take as many of the silver coins that he could carry.

The room behind the last door was full of gold coins and the dog guarding these had eyes as big as towers! But, again, if the soldier lay the apron down, the dog would sit on it while he filled his pockets with the golden coins.

"This is all well and good," the soldier replied. "But nobody gives away treasure for nothing. What do you want in return?"

"The only thing I want is a small tinder box that lies in the room full of gold," the old woman replied.

The soldier agreed to bring her the tinder box. He then climbed down into the hollow of the tree and, when he reached the bottom, it was exactly as the old woman had said. There were three doors directly in front of him.

Behind the first door were chests full of bronze coins and the dog with eyes as big as saucers was guarding them. The soldier placed the old woman's apron on the ground and the dog sat on it, just as she had said it would. He quickly stuffed his pockets full of the coins.

Behind the second door were chests full of silver coins and guarding them was the dog with eyes as big as mill wheels. Again, the soldier lay the apron on the ground and the dog sat on it. Then the soldier emptied his pockets of all the bronze coins and filled them up with silver ones instead.

When he opened the last door, he gasped in astonishment. The room was full of precious, gleaming gold coins. The dog guarding them looked very fierce and really did have eyes as big as towers. The soldier once more laid the apron down and the dog obediently sat on it. The soldier then shook all of the silver coins out of his pockets and filled them up again with as many gold coins as he could carry.

Remembering to pick up the tinder box that lay in the corner of the room, he then climbed out of the hollow tree.

"I see you've done very well for yourself," cackled the old woman, when she saw the soldier's pockets full of the gold coins. "But," she continued, "do you have the tinder box?"

"I most certainly do," replied the soldier. "However, before I give it to you, I would like to know why you want it so much."

"That is a secret," said the old woman.

"Then I will have to kill you and find out the secret for myself," he said. And, before she had a chance to say another word, he took out his sword and cut the old woman's head off.

Then, he put away his sword and went jauntily on his way.

Later that evening, the soldier reached a small town. With his pockets full of money, he stayed in the biggest room of the best inn and ordered the most expensive food and wine.

Over the next few months, he made lots of new friends and gave the most lavish parties.

But, eventually, the money ran out. His friends deserted him and he was forced to move to a cold, shabby attic. On his first night in the attic, he found an old candle which would at least give him a little heat and light. Remembering the old woman's tinder box, he struck it once to light it. There was a puff of smoke and suddenly the dog with the eyes as big as saucers stood before him. The soldier was amazed to see the dog at first, but then thought he might be able to use him.

"Bring me some money!" ordered the soldier.

The dog disappeared and soon returned with a bag full of bronze coins.

When the soldier struck the tinder box twice, the dog with the eyes as big as mill wheels appeared. Once again, the soldier asked him for money, and this time the dog came back with a bag full of silver coins.

When the soldier struck the tinder box three times, the dog with eyes as big as towers appeared. When the soldier asked him for money, he returned with a bag full of gold coins.

The soldier was rich again! He moved into wonderful new lodgings, bought himself the most stylish clothes and lived a life of complete luxury.

One day, he saw the King's beautiful daughter pass by in her carriage. The soldier longed to meet her, but was told that the King never let her out of his sight. So, one night, the soldier struck the tinder box again and, when the dog with eyes as big as saucers appeared, ordered him to bring the King's daughter to him. The dog did as he was told, carrying the sleeping Princess on his back. But a lady-in-waiting had followed the dog to the soldier's lodgings and rushed to the palace to tell the King and Queen what she had seen.

The King and Queen were furious. When they found their daughter in the soldier's lodgings, they had him arrested immediately and ordered that he be executed in the town square.

Early the next morning, the soldier was sitting in his cell, awaiting the dreaded hour, when a small boy's shoe fell through the bars from the street above.
"Can I have my shoe back, please?" asked the boy, peering through the bars.
"Certainly, you can," replied the soldier. "But only if you run to my lodgings and bring me my tinder box which is lying on the table."
The boy rushed off and, not long after, was wearing his shoe again. In his cell, the soldier sat staring at his tinder box with a smile on his face.

A few hours later, the soldier was led up to the scaffold. When he was asked if he had a last request, he replied, "I'd like a final smoke of my pipe."
He put the pipe into his mouth and struck the tinder box once, then twice, then three times. There was a huge puff of smoke and all three dogs appeared, growling, at the soldier's side. On the soldier's order, they ran through the crowds towards the royal party.

The ferocious dogs killed the King and Queen where they stood and many of the courtiers and soldiers, too. Seeing how powerful he was, the people of the town freed the soldier and made him their new King. He married the old King's daughter the very next day.

The soldier was always protected by the three dogs and lived a long life. He kept the tinder box hidden away in the castle vaults so no one would ever be able to take it away from him.

Rumpelstiltskin

O nce upon a time, there was on old woman who lived with her beautiful daughter, Rose, in a run-down old cottage. The woman and the girl were very poor. One day, the old woman happened to see the King riding along the road by her cottage.

"If only I could arrange for the King to meet my daughter," she thought.

She grabbed hold of the King's horse and pulled it to a stop.

"Please, sire, you must meet my daughter. She is very beautiful."

"You stupid woman. Get out of my way before I whip you!" cried the King, nearly falling off his horse.

"But she can do something that would make you very rich," the woman said, desperately trying to hold his attention.

"Oh, and what is that?" asked the King, with curiosity.

The old woman said the first thing that came into her head.

"She can spin straw into gold," she lied.

The King took the old woman's daughter to his castle. He locked her up in a small room that was full of straw. The only other things in the room were a spinning wheel and a small stool.

"Listen to me, Rose," the King began. "I will return in the morning. If all this straw has not been turned into gold, I will chop your pretty little head off!" Then he walked out, locking the door behind him.

Poor Rose was so afraid she started to cry. Just then, she noticed a funny little man with a long, grey beard standing at her elbow.

"What's the matter, my dear?" asked the funny little man.

"My stupid mother told the King that I can spin straw into gold," cried Rose.
If I can't do it, the King will have my head chopped off!"

"What would you give me if I did it for you?" the funny little man asked.

"My necklace," replied Rose, taking it from her neck.

"That will do fine," said the little man, putting it in his pocket. "You have a rest and I'll get on with my work."

The little man sat down and started to spin. The last thing Rose heard before she fell asleep was the whirr of the spinning wheel.

The next morning, Rose awoke. She rubbed her eyes and couldn't believe what she saw. There was no sign of the funny little man, but all the straw in the room had been turned into the finest gold. The King was very pleased when he saw it all.

"You've done very well, Rose," he said. "Now, come with me."

This time he took her to an even bigger room which, again, was full of straw.

"I want all of this spun into gold by the morning, or I'll chop your head off!" threatened the King.

Once again, he left Rose alone in the room and locked the door.
"What am I going to do?" thought Rose, and she began to cry again.
"Don't cry," said a voice at her elbow. "I'll turn it all into gold for you. But what will you give me in return?"
It was the funny little man again, who had just appeared from nowhere!
"Here, take my ring. It was my grandmother's," said Rose.
The little man took the ring, sat at the wheel and began to spin.

The next morning, it was the same as before. The little man had gone and all of the straw had been turned into gold. When the King saw this, he took Rose to a very large room that had straw piled up to the ceiling.

"If you manage to turn all of this into gold, I'll make you my Queen," he said.
"If you don't, it's off with your head!"
After the King had left, the funny little man appeared once more and once more offered to turn all the straw into gold.

"But I have nothing left to give you," said poor Rose.

"There is one thing you can give me. You can give me your first born baby,"
said the little man, slyly.

Rose was so desperate, she agreed to his demand at once.

When the King saw the huge amount of gold in the room the next morning, he
was so pleased that he married Rose immediately. A year later, she gave birth to a
lovely, little baby boy.

In time, Rose forgot about her promise to the little man but, one evening, when
she was all alone nursing her baby, he suddenly appeared at her elbow.

"I have come to claim the baby you promised me," he said, with a cold look in his
eye.

Rose was horrified and promised the little man anything he wanted:
jewels, gold, anything! As long as he didn't take her child away.

The little man thought for a moment and then said, "I will give you a chance to
keep your child. I will come here for the next three nights and each night I will
give you three chances to guess my name. If you don't guess correctly by the third
night, you will never see your baby again."

When the little man appeared on the first night, Rose tried to think of three of
the most unusual names.

"Is it Caspar?" she asked.

"No," replied the little man.

Is it Balthasar?" she asked, anxiously.

"I'm afraid not," he replied with an evil grin.

"What about Melchior?" she asked, even more anxiously.

"Wrong, wrong, wrong!" he cried, gleefully. Then he stamped his foot and disappeared.

The next evening, Rose thought that she'd try more ordinary names.

"Is it John?"

"No," replied the little man.

"Arthur?" she asked again.

"Not even close," he replied.

"How about George?" asked Rose.

"Wrong, wrong, wrong again!" he shouted, happily.

Once again, Rose had failed.

The little man was so pleased that Rose couldn't guess his name, he started to dance around the room with joy.

"If you don't guess my name tomorrow night," he cried, "the child is mine!" Then he stamped his foot and disappeared.

Early the next morning, Rose sent all her servants out to see if they could find anyone who had heard of the little man and knew his name. One by one, the servents came back. They could find no one who had heard of him. Finally, the last servant arrived back and had a strange tale to tell Rose.

Early the next morning, Rose sent all her servants out to see if they could find anyone who had heard of the little man and knew his name. They could find no one who had heard of him. Finally, the last servant arrived back and had a strange tale to tell Rose.

"I was riding through the forest," he said, "and I saw a strange little man with a long, grey beard dancing around his fire. He sang a strange song, too."

"Today I brew, tomorrow I bake. Next day, Queen Rose's baby I'll take.
So I solemnly swear by the hair on my chin, that the name I was given is
Rumpelstiltskin."

Rose was so delighted with this news, she gave the servant a large bag of gold coins as a reward. Later that evening, the little man once again appeared in front of her.
"What are your last three guesses?" he asked Rose, smugly.
"Is it Karl?" she asked.
"No," he replied, happily.
"Umm...Richard?" she asked again.
"Nowhere near, I'm afraid. It's your last guess, Your Majesty, and then the child is mine," the little man said, menacingly.
"Is it...Rumpelstiltskin?"
asked Rose, innocently.
The little man was so
angry that Rose had
guessed his name,
he turned bright blue.
He stamped his foot
down so hard that
he went right
through the floor
and that was
the end of
Rumpelstiltskin.